DEMYSTIFYING MEANING

Structuralism vs. Behaviorism

By MOHAMMED CHIHAB

Demystifying Meaning:

Structuralism vs. Behaviorism

Mohammed Chihab

Copyright © 2017 by Mohammed Chihab

All rights reserved. This book or any portion thereof may not be reproduced or used in any manner whatsoever without permission except for the use of brief quotations in a book review or scholarly journal.

First Published: 2018

ISBN 978-0-9997951-1-8

Published by the Author
authorchihab@gmail.com

*To my sister Sarah, who passed away
in her early childhood.*

Content

Introduction 9

Chapter One: The 'Relational Meaning' with Saussure 16

    SIGNIFIER/SIGNIFIED DICHOTOMY 16

    LANGUE/PAROLE DICHOTOMY 20

    FORM/SUBSTANCE DICHOTOMY................ 25

    SYNTAGMATIC/ PARADIGMATIC RELATIONS. 27

Chapter Two: The 'Non-Linguistic Meaning' with Bloomfield..........................35

    TOWARDS A MECHANISTIC APPROACH........ 35

    TOWARDS A BEHAVIORISTIC MEANING 38

    'MEANING' MATCH OF SPEECH FORMS 45

Chapter Three: General Contrastive Analysis and Comparative study..................47

Conclusion 53

Works Cited 54

Introduction

Semantics, which many linguists and philosophers have harshly criticized, is a main field in linguistics. It is one of the most important areas in which language operates; or rather it can be seen as the central goal and the reason why language as a system does exist. For it would be insane and irrational, if people just speak for the sake of producing sounds that deliver no meaning.

Meaning, thus, is a very important term in linguistics itself. Let us admit that it is very hard to study scientifically. However Bloomfield's attempt to demystify it and make it detectable and discernable is a great move towards providing a scientific representation to it, and he should be praised for that. Others like Saussure, sees meaning as metaphysical but forms a part of the structure. This view contains more of the scientific features to be accounted as valid in linguistics to the study of meaning. If linguistics is defined as the scientific study of language, then it is inappropriate to stand against these theories just for the sake of providing more philosophical ones as substitutes. It is unforgivable to say that for example the behavioristic theory is wrong or full of defects, while it is only an effort to take language to the laboratory.

If structuralism and behaviorism are taken off linguistics, all those works done against them will certainly result in excluding that scientific side of it that should be the dominant one in all of its subfields including semantics.

This book is a contrastive comparative analysis between structuralism with Saussure and behaviorism with Bloomfield towards the study and identification of meaning. The book, then, is divided into three chapters: the first chapter is a review and analysis of Saussure's theory towards 'meaning'. The second one is, also, a review and analysis of Bloomfield's behavioristic theory towards 'meaning'. The last one, which is the third chapter, is a general contrastive comparative analysis between them.

Thus, the objective of the book is to give more importance to scientific approaches. My intention is, thus, understood.

Choosing semantics as a field to write about does not come out of nothing; and it is not against pragmatics and its theories. It is my passion and the requirement to push it forward. It is today that the study of meaning has become a rite for linguists.

Now, this is a small preliminary historical overview that leads us to our topic. For this sake, 19th century comparative philology is considered as the gateway to the 20th century scientific study of language. At this time, philologists deal with meaning from the historical perspective. They study the change of meaning through time.

Comparative philology adopts the way of item-centered-dispatched view, which is a comparison amongst items in different languages or within the same one to establish the continuum model leading to their proto-language or to investigate how certain languages distribute their semantic fields altogether. Take the following languages: French, Spanish and Italian, and let us compare one item in all of them, which is the item 'hand'. In French it is referred to as 'Main', in Spanish as 'Mano', and in Italian as 'Mano'. By more investigation and comparison of items the comparative philologists come to the conclusion that these languages descend from the same mother-language or, in other words, proto-language, which is in our case, the

'Romance' one. This is the reason why hinting to these languages by the Romance languages. For English hand is, as we know, referred to as 'Hand', in German as 'Hand', and in Dutch as 'Hand'. The comparative philologists would, as well, after a deeper investigation and comparison amongst the items, conclude that the languages under scrutiny to be sisters and daughters of the same mother language 'the Proto-Germanic' one. These studies have lead these philologists to draw genealogical trees to classify those languages. Bopp, Humboldt, Grimm are some of those well-known philologists. However, since lexical items can be borrowed or transmitted, somehow and someway, from one language to another and that this phenomenon may lead to confusion and lack of exhaustive analysis, the comparative philologists turn their eyes to the comparison of derivations, for they are based on natural forces and can hardly be borrowed.[1]

Consequently, meaning is seen to have an etymological basis. However, this has been destined to change with the upcoming of 20th century new wave of linguistics, especially with

---

[1] More details about historical linguistics can be found in the books: <u>Historical Linguistics and language change</u> by Roger Lass (1997), <u>Historical Linguistics</u> by Theodora Bynon (1977), and <u>Historical Linguistics</u> by Winfred P. Lehmann (3Ed, 1992).

Saussure. He no longer looks at language from that very narrow vent that limits its study to history. On the other hand, Saussure does not deny the great benefits of comparative philology, but adds that this kind of study is inefficient and insufficient to the investigation of languages. It does not contribute to the representation of what is really going on in them. This point gives rise to language autonomy. For Saussure language should be studied from its structure ignoring time effects and changes. For him, language is complete at every time and every instant, detached from any outside factors. As Frediric Jameson puts it *"Saussure's originality was to have insisted on the fact that language as a total system is complete at every moment, no matter what happens to have been altered in it a moment before." (qtd. in Sless 139).*[2] For Saussure, all languages Are equal and do not need to be compared with others for the sake of investigation. Therefore, the etymological study of language has failed in the identification of the real nature of language, and, then, it has gone wrong in the establishment of a linguistics based on science.

---

[2] Fredric Jameson, 1972, as quoted by Sless David, 1986, In Search of Semiotics.

Saussure focuses on the language structure. He claims that the linguist should study the synchronic relations happening at a certain specific point of time. For example: the sequence 'John congratulated Sue at school before his parents' should be investigated out of time. The item 'John' has paradigmatic relations with the item 'Paul' since they can substitute for each other. John and Paul are then put under scrutiny. For, if Paul did not congratulate Sue, John did. Sue and John are in syntagmatic relations. John comes first in the sequence, which cannot be completed if the one stops at the boundaries of John or congratulated. It, the sequence, should be uttered as whole for the meaning to be caught up and understood. John did not congratulate Julia or Emma, but Sue. Sue, then, is in paradigmatic relations with Julia and Emma. In terms of time, they occur immediately, i.e. at the same moment. However, it is in syntagmatic relations to congratulated, John, at school, and his parents, as it occurs after John and congratulated in the structure, and before the other left items. John congratulated Sue in the past but he is not congratulating her now. The morpheme 'ed' is in a syntagmatic structural relationship to congratulate, and in a paradigmatic relationship to 'is+ing' for the present continuous, or to 'will' for the future. He congratulated her at school, not at home or in the street, and before his parents, not before his father, David, or Janna. He congratulated her before his parents, not before my parents or David's parents. The study takes this pattern getting deeper and deeper in the investigation of the structure. Phonological, morphological and syntactic analyses are all to be handled in the same way.[3] Saussure claims, "Language is a system whose parts can and must all be considered in their synchronic solidarity." (Saussure 87) [4]

---

[3] See F. R. Palmer, Semantics, 1981, for another example and more explanation.

[4] Page references are to the translation of Saussure's Cours de Linguistique Général in General Linguistics, New York, 1959.

Chapter One:
The 'Relational Meaning' with Saussure

1. Signifier/Signified Dichotomy

De Saussure makes a distinction between the terms signifier and signified. The former refers to the form of a given unit in a language and the last to its content. For him, a language unit is a dual entity in which the form (signifier) signifies the content (signified). He claims that, as a system, language is the fundamental basis of communication. He argues that they (the signifier and signified) are not simultaneously occurring. As Hawkes puts it:

> *Since language is fundamentally an auditory system, the relationship between signifier and signified unfolds during a passage of time [...] In short, the mode of the relationship between [them] can be said to be essentially, albeit minimally, sequential in nature. (Hawkes 25)* [5]

Thus, the signifier (form) precedes the signified (content) in time and it signifies it. He considers the relation that holds amongst them as conventional and arbitrary.

For Saussure, the form 'tree' has nothing to do with the real down-to-earth tree that grows out in the wilds or nature in general. It does not illustrate it as it is with branches and leafs. It is completely different from the real tree that is planted in somebody's garden or out in the forest. There is, ultimately, no necessary link between signs and the physical world. Their relation is only a question of arbitrary decision. However, in real

---

[5] Terence, Hawkes. <u>Structuralism and Semantics</u>. 1977.

onomatopoeia this regulation is somehow constrained and slightly no more valid. The name given to refer to a birdcall may, to a certain extent, match the form-sound set for it. There exists maybe some sort of connection that, somehow and someway, links them together. Nonetheless, onomatopoeia is untenable across systems and remains generally language specific. 'Cock-a-doodle-doo' is a term used to spot the cock-call in English. However, in French it is named 'cocorico', which is very much different. This would make it indiscernible to perceive and sketch within the foreign system except for locals who speak that language and who may be able to make the contrast clear amongst them. Thus, onomatopoeia itself varies across systems. The English system may have a bit slightly different onomatopoeic forms from the French or Chinese ones and, thus, remains culture specific (i.e. not universal). The system is internalized within the minds of the community members, and therefore leaves no room for the decisions of individuals.

The Signifier and signified form a single unit. This unit is the sign. According to Saussure, language is a system of signs, and the sign is fundamental to the existence of language, and constitutes its basis. Thus, for him, *"Signs are what linguistics studies" (Saussure 102).* Since the sign is largely arbitrary and conventional, it cannot be negotiated or discussed. As De Saussure puts it, *"any subject to be discussed must have a reasonable basis" (Saussure 73).* The notion of arbitrariness does not possess the quality of reasonability to be taken ahead in discussion. No one would ever go and reconsider the factual relation holding between the signifier and signified of a certain unit.

For, Saussure, a sign may incorporate within itself other sings. The number seventy-three is a sign that contains, within itself, two other incorporated signs, which are seventy and three. This complex sign is considered as a cumulative sign and is more significant, and, thus, a whole text containing a number of signs is to be taken as a cumulative sign. Here, as Saussure theorized, I would argue that a whole chapter is itself a sign containing a number of single and complex signs. It is a cumulative sign that is made up of a bunch of single signs. However, the cumulative sign is never a third part in carrying a cumulative content (signified).

Signs operate amongst each other and form a system. This system is broken up into two main categories: a mother and daughter category. The mother category is what we call in English 'language' in general, and the daughter category is what we, again, call in English 'speech'. Saussure has developed two concepts to refer to both categories. The first is 'langue' which refers to language in general as a system of interrelated signs in their ideal state, and the second is 'parole' which refers to speech as the sum total of utterances individuals actually produce. It is the concrete representation of language in real conditions or rather in real life. 'Langue' is incomplete within individual speakers. It is only complete in society. It is a social fact out of which the individual selects what to say to perform in the concrete world. These selections are what Saussure calls 'parole'.

2. Langue/Parole Dichotomy

We have seen how Saussure accounts for the dichotomy 'signifier vs. signified', and the relationship he establishes between signs and language, i.e. a system of interrelated signs that hang together and condition one another.

Structuralism is essentially founded upon the concept of 'langue'. A term developed by Saussure to refer to the *'language system'* in a broad sense rather than the *'actual speech'*. As he deals with speech as prior to writing, he deals with 'langue' as prior to 'parole' *(Usó-Juan 7)*[6]. 'Langue' is the property of the collectivity as opposed to 'parole', which is the property of the individual. 'Langue' allows for a proper account of language. It is defined as the language system. It is the set of rules and principles that lie behind every utterance produced by the speaker and understood by the listener. It is a common and shared knowledge by both. It resides in both of them and enables them to communicate. 'Parole' is, on the other hand, a product of the individual. It is active as opposed to 'langue', which is passive. It is the sum total of all utterances that individuals have ever produced. In his description of 'parole', Harland noted that *"he [De Saussure] argued that 'langue' should take precedence over 'parole', i.e. that the system of language in general should take precedence over the sum*

---

[6] Esther, Usó-Juan et al. Current Trend in the Development and Teaching of the four language skills. Mouton de Guyter: Berlin, 2006.

total of all the actual utterances ever actually uttered" (Harland 11).[7] Here, Harland provides us with a definition of 'parole' and establishes a preference of 'langue' over it as Saussure maintains in his analysis.

Saussure offers a good analogy to account for language, which he compares to the chess game. The chessboard and its pions are all seen as a system, and whoever wants to play the game must bring with him a prior knowledge about conventional rules and principles that govern the whole game. He has to study the game from the angle of the sum total of all the chess games ever carried out before. It would be absurd and has no-concrete account of the chess as a game if the player does not consider it as a related system and that every move he takes is an assortment made out of a collection of potential moves. The moves are taken ahead along with a simultaneous system of rules and principles that cover each one made by the players collectively, not by each one individually. This simultaneous system is the mother source of every move throughout the game and playtime. It is what allows players to take

---

[7] Richard, Harland. <u>Super Structuralism: The Philosophy of Structuralism and Post-Structuralism</u>. 1987.

moves ahead systematically in accordance with the sum total of all the moves ever made. It is a sort of knowledge which lies behind every single move at every single moment. Therefore, it is collectively installed in the consciousness of the players to help them establish a unified system that operates in a way to make them hold the play.

This model matches the nature of language in that the two systems apply the same game quirks. Within language as a system of interrelated signs, 'Langue' comes first prior to any actual concrete utterances. It is the abstract ideal level of language. The selected utterance or signal is related to a bunch of possible alternative replacements out of which a speaker may choose what to utter. What lies behind speech performance is 'langue'. It is what enables the speaker to become aware of his world. Out of 'langue', humans are but animals that live outside following their instinct. 'Langue' contains the knowledge of the world of a certain society. It is a kind of abstract stock of language in its ideal form, more powerful than the individual who can never create or produce new utterances or meanings. Everyone should recognize his nature before his involvement in his society; otherwise he will never become part of it and remain alien or a 'freaky intruder'. For instance, an immigrant always finds it difficult to be accepted and assimilated within a community, if the 'langue' of his origins is not similar to the one he is immigrating to. His language would sound different and problematic, or, if accepted, it would sound some kind of art or poetic way of talking. Sub-Saharan Africans, when they come to Morocco, their French is fully noticed. The way they speak, or choose utterances makes it obvious that they are not Moroccans but refugees. This is similar to Middle-Eastern people when they, also, come to Morocco; they find it difficult to understand what a Moroccan is saying, although they may be using Arabic terms. What is internalized in a Moroccan mind is different from what is internalized in an Emirati for example. Societies are different, and since 'langue' is a social fact, it is really hard for 'parole' to match, and then understanding one another would be awkward.

'Parole' is the personal style, that part of language which is determined by the rules and constraints imposed by 'langue' on it. Thus, 'langue' is a sort of contract accepted by all members of a community. Whether they like or not, they sign it, adopt it, and use it. It is a social fact as Saussure puts it, *"[Langue] is the social side of speech, outside the individual who can never create or modify it by himself; it exists only by virtue of a sort of contract signed by the members of the community"* (Saussure 14).

Meaning is never complete at the level of the utterance alone, but only in relation to 'langue'. The tissue of language is made up of relations. The meaning of "my dog" when I refer to it in the following sentence: 'My dog is quite smart' does not reside within the dog itself, but in the notion of dogness that resides in an abstract form in 'langue'. It derives its meaning from an ideal and perfect dog that refers to all dogs before the concrete world, i.e. a concept. This takes us right to the dichotomy that language is form not substance.

3. Form/Substance Dichotomy

Language is form not substance. Saussure claims that language is a system of interrelated items that co-exist together and condition one another. Items have no significance in themselves, but derive their meaning from other items of the same system. In this respect, Hawkes writes, *"it [language] is a structure which has modes, rather than an aggregate of items which has content"* (Hawkes 28).

If the monetary system is taken as an analogy, it reveals the major characteristics of language as a system but not a substance. The metal out of which a Moroccan coin of 10DH is made or its quantity may not, if taken out of the system, match the 10DH price when purchased. From here, we notice that the value of the coin does not reside in itself as a material or, if using Saussure's term, as a substance, but derives it when used and compared with other coins within the monetary system.

Saussure gives another analogy to the fact that language is form not substance. This analogy is that of chess game. First, if two chess games are held in different places one on board of a ship sailing in the Mediterranean Sea and the other somewhere in Canada, this would not change anything in the game itself as it would be held the same way. Second, if a chess board and its pieces are made of gold, while the other one's are made of ivory, this would, also, change nothing of the game. Third, if within the golden board and pieces a knight pion is broken and replaced by a wooden one, this changes nothing of the game itself. This implies that the game is not governed by the place where it is held, or by the shapes or the substance of its board and pieces. Provided that the rules and principles of the play are set, understood, and respected, the game can be played everywhere, using whatever shape of board and pieces. What counts are the rules and principles that underlie and govern the game. The value of the chess board or its pieces does not reside in their substance but in the relations that hold amongst them.

This structure perfectly applies to language. The implication of such analogies is that language is form not substance in which it is realized. Here, form refers to the relations that a certain language imposes upon the underlying substance.

4. Syntagmatic/Paradigmatic Relations

As we have already mentioned before, signs are always in relations amongst themselves. They operate synchronically according to the type of relation that holds at one moment. All linguistic signs come into these kinds of associations which Saussure calls paradigmatic and syntagmatic relations.

Saussure claims that a pion of chess is an empty and useless entity in itself. It derives its significance only from its relation to other pieces on the board and how it can function in association to them. The same operates within language. Saussure puts it as following:

> *The concepts are purely differential and defined not by their positive content but negatively by their relations with the other terms of the system. Their most precise characteristic is in being what the others are not. (Saussure 117)*

Saussure is clear and precise in defining this feature of language. Syntagmatic relations happen linearly among adjacent items within the same sequence of signs. For him, a syntagm is a successive chain of units that may be phonemes, morphemes, syllables, expressions, etc. These items derive their informational value from one another not signs themselves taken separately. The adjacent ones contribute to their context. Thus, they are hollow until they are taken within the syntagm as whole. The components of a syntagm are co-present and co-referential. Therefore, these Syntagmatic relations are referred to as relations in presentia. For example, take the morphemes 'un' and 'clear', and join them together. Here, both morphemes will form the syntagm 'unclear' in which their relations are in presentia. The item 'un' will certainly contribute to the reversion of the meaning of the other component 'clear'. They form a sequence where each one rests on the existence of the other.

'Can' is a verb that can play different roles depending on the structure in which it is used. In the sentence 'Lucy can drive', 'can' is an auxiliary verb referring to Lucy's ability and knack to drive something like a car or motorcycle or whatever else. In the sentence 'The Darwins can turkey', 'can' is a main verb referring to the process of putting turkey into cans. What determines the formational value of 'can' is not the way it is pronounced since it has the same sound properties, but the other items it is used with. What defines 'can' as an auxiliary verb is its neighbor the item 'drive'. In the other case, what identifies the word 'can' as a main verb is again its neighbor the item turkey. Thus, the syntagmatic relations play a vital role in the identification of each component's informational value.

Unlike syntagmatic relations, paradigmatic relations are substitutional associations amongst the items of the syntagm and those existing in 'langue'. They are relations in opposition amongst those capable of taking the structural position of those present within the sintagm; it holds amongst the linguistic elements that can possibly occur in the same milieu. For Saussure, a paradigm is any vertical linguistic field where items are of the same kind and can substitute for one another. These relations are called relations in absentia, for they hold amongst elements present within the syntagm and those present at the level of 'langue' but absent in it. Since it (the syntagm) is made of the selections the one chooses, it has the nature feature of 'parole'. The paradigmatic relations contribute in a very serious way to the identification of meaning after the sintagmatic ones.

The example given by Terence Hawkes can be of a good value to count for this kind of relations. He writes, *"Yet it is also clear that what makes any single item 'meaningful' is not its own particular quality, but the difference between this quality and that of other sounds"*, the quality of human sounds contribute to meaning construction and differentiation, *"In fact the differences are systematised into 'oppositions' which are linked in crucial relationships" (Hawkes 22).*

Hawkes studies the words 'tin' and 'kin' to provide a clear account for this. The initial sound of both words is what makes them different in meaning from each other. The sound of /t/ is having dissimilar qualities from those characterizing the sound of /k/. Thus, the contrast is registered within the language from these qualities that helps produce meaning. *(Hawkes 22)*

If the one takes account of phonology, /k/ and /t/ are phonologically different as for the phonemes /b/ and /p/ in 'big' and 'pig'. /b/ and /p/ occur within the same context /-ig/. They can substitute for each other. At this primary phonemic level words get their meaning paradigmatically. When the speech sound /b/ is substituted for /p/, the one will subsequently get the word 'big' that refers to something large, more extended, or powerful. However, when reversed, the one will get 'pig' which refers to a heavy and large animal with tiny short legs and a twisted tail. In English they are both in complementary distribution, which allows them to produce meaning. This quality of being two separate phonemes is what distributes meaning to each context.

However, in the case of free variation, two forms or more can carry the same meaning. Example from Moroccan Arabic, /qal/ and /gal/ are two words that refer to the same action; they both mean 'said' or rather represent the verb say in its past form. Although, they take the same context, meaning is still never altered.

Therefore, the significance of the phonemes is not always registered by language, since it makes no difference. Only a small proportion of such kind is recognized, and is put under consideration to produce meaning in this way. *"In fact, large numbers of contrasts are ignored by it, and only a relatively small proportion of the differences that actually occur between sounds are recognised as different for the purpose of forming words and creating meaning" (Hawkes 23).* For example in the case of minimal pairs, the contrast between the phonemes is of less importance and ignored by language in the distribution of meaning.

Such ignorance occurs, for example, in the words 'light' and 'flight'. They, both, represent a minimal pair. However, language does not need to spot the difference between the sound /l/ as it occurs in 'light' and /l/ in 'flight'. Phonemically they are not the same, but language does not show the distinction. The speech sound /f/ is the one that plays the role of the distinctive contrastive element between the words. Thus, the focus would be cast upon it instead of the sound /l/ as it appears in both words.

In 'flight', the word is having an extra-feature that the word 'light' does not have. However, in the words 'fight' without the sound /l/ and in the word 'light', the words express two main dissimilar meanings. They are two distinctive contrastive speech sounds, or in other words, they are two separate phonemes and, thus distribute two different contents.

In the words flight, fight and light, the meaning is distributed according to paradigmatic relations that hold amongst the sounds /fl/, /f/, and /l/. They can operate oppositionally, and substitute for each other within the context /-ight/.

Meaning, thus, is restored not from the word itself but oppositionally in relation to those words present in the utterance, as Saussure's example points at, *"it is impossible to fix even the value of the word "sun" without first considering its surroundings: in some languages it is not possible to say, "Sit in the sun""* (Saussure 116), and those absent from the utterance but present in 'langue'.

Saussure stresses his view upon language that it is a structure made up of relations. These relations are of two kinds; syntagmatic relations that hold amongst the units of language horizontally within the syntagm, and paradigmatic relations that happens vertically and oppositionally. For him, language can be accounted for in terms of these relations. Thus, meaning is relational not substantial.

Chapter Two:
The 'Non-Linguistic Meaning' with Bloomfield

1. Towards a mechanistic Approach

The descriptivist school is founded by Franz Boas. But Leonard Bloomfield (1887-1949) is the one to fame its quirks. The main points Boas treated is handled but rather elucidated and much elaborated by Bloomfield. He, Bloomfield, has become the leading figure of this school and is well-known amongst scholars. He has studied linguistics in the traditional fashion. However, in contrary to his uncle Maurice Bloomfield, his inclination and passion are particularly devoted to synchronic linguistics to leave reliable literature in the study of American Indian languages. He has published two interesting books in the history of linguistics. In 1914 he published his book 'Introduction to the study of Language', and then in 1933 he published his famous book 'Language' where he discusses the physics and identity of language. Here, he presents his behavioristic theory. However, this last book is in fact only a revision to his earlier published book.

Behaviorism is first initiated in psychology. J. B. Watson is the one to set up its grounds. His 1925 publication of his book 'Behaviorism' is considered the main gateway to the approach. This book was revised to be in the hand of the public once more in 1930. It handles the notion of behavior in general. However, the reader encounters two special sections while reading it Watson dedicates to the study of the linguistic behavior, in which he questions the relationship between language and thinking. He refutes the mental property of language, especially what is known as conscience. He limits his view to what is observable, measurable, and detectable. Language, for him, is a collection of linguistic habits the individual acquires from his environment and which is no different from other behaviors. From this principle, he defines language as the situation in which it occurs (Watson)[8].

The behavioristic approach, thus, is concerned with the study of behavior and the physics of language. This does tightly reflect Bloomfield's attitudes towards the nature of study that should be adopted by linguists. He tries his best to drive linguistics ahead towards autonomy and science. He is mainly affected by the behaviorist psychological theorist Albert Weiss. He deals primarily and only with what is observable and measurable to define the nature of language.

For him, human conduct is part of stimulus-response, cause-and-effect sequences, which does perfectly matches the basic characteristics of physics and chemistry. Thus, all the abstract psychological and linguistic features do not fit within the behavioristic framework, for which there is no scientific evidence or empirical investigation. He claims that the language can be described exclusively by cause-affect dichotomy, and what cannot be observed and measured has no relevance

---

[8] J. B. Watson, Behaviorism. New York: People's Institute, 1924.

and should be left out of the linguist's task towards language.

Thus, the behavioristic theory ignores the internal mental side in favor of the environment. The Behaviorists consider the internal side as *'inaccessible to proper scientific investigation' (Williams and Robert 8)*[9].

2. Towards a Behavioristic 'Meaning'

The Watson's definition of stimulus may perfectly explicate the core of the theory. He maintains that stimulus is anything in the environment or any transformation in the physiological condition of the animal that escorts to some form of behavior. Based on this definition, Bloomfield works out his behavioristic account for the nature of language. He maintains that speech is merely a form of behavior that is conditioned by the stimulus and the response it activates, and thus language can be presented in terms of this dichotomy. For him, constructive generalizations about language are merely 'inductive' generalizations. Thus, the definition

---

[9] **Marion, Williams, and Burden L. Robert, 1997, Psychology for Language Teachers. Cambridge University Press.**

of meaning in the behavioristic view has been tight and limited. As J. D. Fodor describes it, *"The meaning of an expression is said to be [...] the stimuli which elicit utterances of it and/or the behavioral responses it evokes" (Fodor 13).* [10]

Bloomfield is, thus, defining 'meaning' as the situation in which language is used. He offers quite a contrast between speech events and practical events to account for his view, which will be illustrated and made clear in his little following story about Jack and Jill walking down the lane. Jill sees an apple. She is hungry. With the use of her sounds coming out of her vocal tract she gets Jack, who hears her, to climb the tree and fetch it for her.

If nobody including jack had been there, or if she had been an animal, she would have received a 'stimulus' (S) that would have activated a 'response' (R). She would have gone, climbed the tree, and got the apple. The course of events would have been diagrammed as following:

---

[10]**Dean Janet, Fodor. <u>Semantics: Theories of Meaning in Generative Grammar</u>. Harvester Press, 1980.**

The stimulus would have activated a response in a situation where no act of speech have had occurred. The behavior would have included only practical events.

Since Jack was there with her, the stimulus (S) activated a linguistic response (r) instead of a practical reaction (R). Jill made sounds using her vocal tract, which is the act of speech. The sound waves produced a stimulus for Jack, which is a linguistic stimulus (s). Jack, in his turn, went and fetched the apple, which is a non-linguistic reaction, but a practical one (R) to the linguistic stimulus. This can be diagrammed as following:

$$S \longrightarrow r \ldots\ldots\ldots\ldots s \longrightarrow R$$

The story can be broken down into:

a)
> Practical (Real-world) events preceding the act of speech as shown by (S).

b)
> Speech (Spoken) as shown by (r) and (s).

c)
> Practical (Real-world) events following the act of speech as shown by (R).

Scientifically the stimulus and response are interpreted as physical events. The light falls ahead on the apple, it gets reflected directly to Jill's eyes. She analyzes the information with her nervous system. The pain in her stomach is more received. The nervous system, then, orders to the muscles of her vocal tract to produce sounds. Jack's response to the sound waves is no-less physical.

As his inclination is scientific, Bloomfield was even to reject the study of meaning. He claims that the study of meaning is impossible and out of man. As it is obscure and has no physics, it cannot be observed or measured. Thus, it should be left outside the range of linguistic study, and there may be other science which has the ability to handle the notion of meaning that can be defined according to it. Bloomfield states, "The statement of meaning is therefore the weak point in language-study and will remain so until human knowledge advances very far beyond its present state. In practice, we define the meaning of a linguistic form [...] in terms of some other science" (Bloomfield 140).[11]

Then, the behavioristic theory has been very precise to take the notion of meaning

---

[11] **Leonard, Bloomfield. <u>Language</u>. 1933.**

from a highly obscure, murky, and abstract state to something that we can contain and effortlessly handle. All those abstract notions like love, hate and joy are all far from being controlled and examined, and thus the study of their meaning will set forth a problematic issue to the principles of the theory. Here, the familiarization of meaning, which is held by the behavioristic theory, is broken into something else more demystified and concrete. In his criticism of the referential, ideational, and behavioristic theory, J. D. Fodor notes:

> *[...]. In this form, these theories are intended as answers to the second question, the question about what meaning really is. The desire to make this move is understandable, especially when what meaning is identified with something relatively familiar and unproblematic.* (Fodor 13)

If we analyze the move to disseminate meaning, we will find out that it has taken three dimensions: The first is that of the refutation of the study of meaning as holding problematic abstract properties and for to be investigated by other specialized science. The second is the salvation attempt to the situation by containing it, and letting aside those abstract notions as having no physics or patterns, and thus unempirical. The third is the provision of relevant substitution, which is the study of behavior as a strong representative for meaning. Bloomfield says, *"We have defined the meaning of a linguistic form as the situation in which the speaker utters it and the response which it calls forth in the hearer"* (Bloomfield 139).

For Jack to react to Jill's linguistic stimulus is no different from being physical, as Bloomfield's view is that speech is part of human behavior, and that for him, human behavior is controlled by the same physical and deterministic laws the same as the other events in the world.

However, even the response, for Bloomfield, depends on predisposing factors, which can be interpreted in term of readiness to a particular stimulus. Bloomfield does not deny the existence of what are non-physical, abstract, and internal processes, such as feelings, thoughts, images, etc, but described them as popular terms related to bodily movements, which are the property of the individual that can be the only one aware of. Thus, Jill would not have acted that way if her relationship to Jack had not been intact or that closer, and jack would have not responded to go and fetch the apple if he had had hard-feelings towards her. For the situation, thus, to have been happened in all these conditions, was important and indispensable. The entire life history of the speaker and hearer creates predisposing factors that would govern the practical events. Thus, the linguistic response may occur in exactly the same at different situations, which reflect the great importance of predisposing factors to make for. For instance, I am hungry may occur even after having a good-birthday party by someone who has eaten a lot of cake and does not want for the party to finish up.

Bloomfield, also, uses science to define the meaning of a speech form accurately for things about which the world has empirical and concrete representations. He says, "We can define the meaning of a speech-form accurately when this meaning has to do with some matter of which we possess scientific knowledge" (Bloomfield 139).

He gives the example of 'salt' to support his claim. He provided its chemical representation, which is 'sodium chloride (NaCl)' as the meaning for it.

3. Meaning match of Speech Forms

Till now, the theory has been discussed from within its framework and its content. Now, it is time to put an investigative eye on it to measure up one of its pivot applications, the 'meaning match of speech forms'. What does this expression really carry within itself and for the theory?

The demystification of meaning is important to the theory to provide principles and rules. The first principle is that meaning is the situation and the response that it calls forth. The second principle is that the linguist can provide meaning to a speech form which he possesses some scientific knowledge about. The third principle is meaning match of speech forms.

The third principle depends solely on the first one in its function, and it can easily be interpreted in J. D. Fodor words, "The theory does predict that two expressions mean the same if they are evoked by the same stimuli and/or elicit the same responses" (Fodor 13).

This shows that if many speech forms are somehow produced as a result of the same stimulus and within the same situation, and/or if they bring down the same response, these speech forms, then, carry the same meaning. Here, that is why I am making use of the expression 'meaning match of speech forms' to represent the principle in a more compressed way.

Chapter Three:
General Contrastive Analysis and Comparative study

Meaning has taken different forms across structuralism and behaviorism depending on their definitions of the nature of language. De Saussure defines language as a system of interrelated items, built on rules, relations, and principles. He adopts the relational definition of language and rejects the substantial one that has existed before. Thus, he claims that meaning is, therefore, structure. Bloomfield, on the other hand, adopts the structuralistic approach and method to analyze language, but he implements a behavioristic view in his identification of the nature of language. For him, since linguistics is a scientific discipline and that defining the meaning of abstract thoughts, ideas, and linguistic forms is far from reach and being held in the linguistic laboratory with observation and field investigation, it should be put aside and let other science handles it. Accordingly, he makes up for that by the study of 'non-linguistic meaning'. For him, meaning is behavior, or, using his terms, "the meaning of a linguistic form [is] *the situation in which the speaker utters it and the response which it calls forth in the hearer*" *(Bloomfield 139)*.

From above, it is understood that De Saussure used a metaphysical approach to identify and study language, since his notion 'langue' has abstract features. It is the ideal level of language, which he defends and supports to be its perfect state which the linguist is supposed to study and draw conclusions from. On the other hand, Bloomfield performs on linguistics with no attempt to use any psychological, sociological, metaphysical or even semantic features in his definition and characterization of language. His notions, situation and response, are of behavioristic nature, and has nothing to do with any abstract level or phase. Basel Al-

Sheikh Hussein, in his comparison between De Saussure and Bloomfield's views, writes:

> *American linguistics differs essentially form de Saussure's structuralism since this underlies a deductive method. De Saussure influenced linguistics merely formally. This means, linguistic units are according to de Saussure not determined on the level of parole as the concrete act of speaking, but on that of the "linguistic system" (the corresponding term in de Saussure is "langue"). (Al-Sheikh Hussein 37 - 39)[12]*

De Saussure contains meaning in structure. He limits the identification and study of language in all its parts into a relational

---

[12] Basel, Al-Sheikh Hussein. "Leonard Bloomfield's View of Structuralism and Linguistics". <u>Global Journal of social human science</u>. volume XII, Issue II, Version I, January 2012

theory. Conversely, Bloomfield considers this attempt as deficient. So, he adopts a double-faced theory. For him, there must be a theory that does not take into account only systematic relational aspects of language to its study and description, but which also takes other ones, and, then, he provides his double-faced view that takes of structuralism as a method to analyze language and of behavior to define its nature.

Structuralism and behaviorism has both neglected the social side of language that some scholars, like Hudson, have come to defend.

As a result meaning for Bloomfield has nothing to do with consciousness or unconsciousness. If the one thinks deliberately of something and utters it, while the situation and the response it evokes are different, this means that its meaning is different, since what counts is behavior.

The description of the meaning of a linguistic form differs from the structuralistic to the behavioristic theory. As has noted previously, if meaning is structure for De Saussure, it is the situation and behavioral response for Bloomfield. This leads to remarkably dissimilar roads to seeking the identity of linguistic forms.

For structuralism, the word 'dog' which I use to refer to my pet is actually deduced from the most perfect 'dog' that exists in the ideal form and level of language as a concept, and which represents all 'dogs' that exists in reality in their various shapes and kinds. The 'meaning' of the word 'tree' that stands in our street near home does not reside in itself but is deduced in relation to the most perfect 'tree' that only exists as a concept in the ideal form, which is langue.

However, Bloomfield does not take meaning to the abstract level. He keeps it concrete, observable, and most of all detectable. Thus, the meaning of the word 'dog' would vary from situation in which it is uttered to another, and/or from response which it calls forth in the hearer to another. If a family is sitting at a restaurant and a child utters the word 'dog', it does not implies the dog he keeps at home, but rather in this situation, since his father has given him pizza, and as a reaction he refuses it, and starts saying 'dog'. His mom goes away and brings him a 'hot dog' plate, which is a meal made to be eaten. Meaning of the linguistic form he utters is, thus, the situation in which it occurs and the response resulting as a consequence.

For a structuralistic view, if two linguistic forms have the same structure, it means they are equal and deliver the same 'meaning'. On the other hand, for a behavioristic view, if two linguistic forms are uttered within similar situations and activate similar responses, it means they are equal and deliver the same 'meaning'.

For a structuralistic view, again, if two linguistic forms are uttered within similar situations and elicits similar responses but have different structures, it means that they are not equal and do not offer the same 'meaning'. For a behavioristic view, if two linguistic forms have similar structures but are uttered within dissimilar situations and have dissimilar responses, it means that they are not equal and do not deliver the same 'meaning'.

Conclusion

'Meaning', as seen before, has taken two kinds of definitions. However, here, we are not looking for a perfect and ideal representation to it as much as we are looking for a scientific one. Let aside all the philosophical ones and bring down to study everything controllable, such as the principles adopted by behaviorism.

In the study and comparison we have taken earlier, there is a large quantity of proofs that support the theories under study to reflect real life. For instance, through behavior you can understand if your request is being accepted or refused, or if your child is making sense of your language. Even if structuralism goes further than enough from reality, it is still valid as it is a good way to establish the link between the study of meaning and the scientific definition of linguistics.

Thus, the structuralist and behaviorist theories fit properly within linguistics and participate perfectly in its evolution and development.

Works cited

Bloomfield, Leonard. Language. New York: Holt, 1933.

Bynon, Theodora. Historical Linguistics. New York: Cambridge University Press, 1977.

Fodor, Janet Dean. Semantics: Theories of Meaning in Generative Grammar. Harvester Press, 1980.

Harland, Richard. Super Structuralism: The Philosophy of Structuralism and Post- Structuralism. London and New York: Routledge, 1987.

Hawkes, Terence. Structuralism and Semantics .Berkeley and Los Angeles: The University of California Press, 1977.

Hussein Al-Sheikh, Basel. "Leonard Bloomfield's View of Structuralism and Linguistics". Global Journal of social human science, volume XII, Issue II, Version I, January 2012 <https://globaljournals.org/GJHSS_Volume12/5-Leonard-Bloomfields-View-of-Structuralism-and-Linguistics.pdf>

Lass, Roger. <u>Histrical Linguistics and Language Change</u>. London: Cambridge University Press, 1997.

Lehmann, P. Winfred. Historical Linguistics. 3Ed. London: Routledge, 1992.

Palmer, R. F. Semantics. 1981.

Saussure, De Fernand. <u>Course in General Linguistics</u>. Ed. Charles Bally and Albert Sechehaye, in collaboration with Albert Reidlinger, Trans. Wade Baskin, New York: The Philosophical Library, 1959.

Sless, David. <u>In Search of Semiotics</u>. 1986.

Usó-Juan, Esther, et al. <u>Current Trend in the Development and Teaching of the four language skills</u>. Mouton de Guyter: Berlin, 2006.

Watson, B. J. <u>Behaviorism</u>. New York: People's Institute, 1924.

Williams, Marion and Robert L. Burden. <u>Psychology for languge teachers</u>. Cambridge: Cambridge University Press, 1997.

www.ingramcontent.com/pod-product-compliance
Lightning Source LLC
Chambersburg PA
CBHW022110160426
43198CB00008B/425